WWW.IAMWOMANNETWORK.COM

# I Said YES

Driven Entrepreneurs Who Overcame
Setbacks, Fear, Failure, & Limitations

16 Driven Entrepreneurs in
Collaboration with
## Yakinea Marie

I SAID YES
Copyright © 2017 Yakinea Marie
All rights reserved.

ISBN: 978-1974102624

**IAWN Publishing**
1710 – 2nd Avenue N, Suite 209
Birmingham, AL 35203

---

All rights reserved. No part of this publication may be reproduced for the purpose of financial gain. Brief quotations may be copied and used for the purpose of personal and organizational study and encouragement without the prior permission of the publisher. Upon request permission will be given if deemed viable.

---

For more information on upcoming events, speaking engagements, or life coaching visit:

www.IAmWomanNetwork.com
www.YakineaMarie.com

To connect with the co-authors visit:
**www.ISaidYes.biz**

# Contents

| | |
|---|---|
| Foreword | 7 |
| Dedication | 9 |
| **Yakinea Marie** | 13 |
| ~ Living Outside The Box of Average | |
| **Curtis K Richardson** | 21 |
| ~ Embracing Your Identity | |
| **Mona Lisa Morris** | 29 |
| ~ From Start to *Finish College Smart*™ | |
| **Mishondy Wright-Brown** | 37 |
| ~ Childlike Faith | |
| **Joe Lockett** | 45 |
| ~ Fear | |
| **Melva Tate** | 53 |
| ~ Build Your Team & Circle The Wagons! | |
| **Mary Sood** | 65 |
| ~ Kissing Your Excuses Goodbye | |
| **Jakim L. Jackson** | 75 |
| ~ Consistency | |
| **SL Stoutermire** | 81 |
| ~ Stay Within Your Gifts and Talents | |

**Linda H. Lee**      91
~ Resilience

**Ferlando Parker Sr.**      99
~ Trust The Process

**Juarkena Pitts**      107
~ From Ministry to the Marketplace

**Danielle Evans**      117
~ Every Decision Matters

**Ronda A. White**      125
~ The Power of Prayer – A Quiet Mind

**Cassandra Goodman**      135
~ Overcoming Struggle with a Changed Mindset

**Tamiko Kelley**      143
~ Trusting In My Source And Not My Resources

**Jacqueline Battle**      151
~ Destiny and Decisiveness,
My Destiny Is In My Hands!

# Foreword

I am honored to have been asked to contribute to this collection of short stories drafted by a phenomenal group of entrepreneurs who are all accomplished, wise, assertive, and successful. Each author discloses the challenges faced during their journey, not because they are seeking accolades and pats on the back, but rather the obstacles they overcame, how they persevered and learned from mistakes and missteps. As I've read these stories, I am reminded of a piece I wrote for my radio program, "Fear is the Enemy of Entrepreneurship." In that vignette, I referenced 2nd Timothy where the Bible says, "For God has not given us a spirit of fear, but of power and of love and of a sound mind." Power to produce the energy required to run a successful venture, love for people, customers and employees and the smarts, the wherewithal, the discipline to produce and provide for themselves their families and their community.

I've never known a really successful business owner who was fearful. Quite the contrary is true, from my experience. Successful businessmen and businesswomen, like the ones featured here are courageous, and more often than not, daring. As one author will tell you, the ability to continue to press forward, sometimes against the tide, is a product of our beliefs. Belief in one's self, the idea, the technique, the product and the service even when you are the only person who believes in your business and your dream. Most importantly, belief that God has ordered the steps you are taking and that he will be with you through triumph and tribulation.

All businesses and business owners have ups and downs, growing pains, and dilemmas. As you read this book, you'll note that these authors were not immune to challenges but in each and every case those challenges were met. One storyteller reminds us that in order to be successful one must be both patient and resilient. Succeeding in a venture is not guaranteed to happen quickly or easily and the surest way to ensure failure is to quit.

Another writer advises that trust is key. Trust in God and in the idea. Still others talked about the importance of strategic preparation and planning. This collection also reinforces the principles like, "every decision matters" and you must "embrace your identity."

So, I congratulate all the writers and contributors to the "I Said Yes Collaboration". I'd be remiss if I failed to acknowledge the leader of this effort, Yakinea Marie Duff who encouraged these trailblazers and who has diligently worked to help others succeed.

**Bob Dickerson**
Executive Director
Birmingham Business Resource Center

# *Dedication*

This book is dedicated to every person who has said YES to moving forward in the pursuit of their dream, vision, or idea in hopes of making it a successful reality. Anyone can talk about what they are going to do or even quit when times get tough. But those who are willing to put consistent actions to their words and are determined to win regardless of the setback or obstacle are to be celebrated and commended.

I celebrate you because you are the standard. You are the example that aspiring and current entrepreneurs need to see in the marketplace. You are extraordinary. You are uncommon. You are a driven entrepreneur who said YES!!!

A special thanks to everyone who made the "I Said Yes" Book Collaboration possible: my business mentor and Foreword Bob Dickerson, book coordinator Juarkena Pitts, graphic designer Alicia Watts, editor Thirley Ross, and every participating author.

*~Yakinea Marie*

I AM
DRIVEN

# Living Outside The Box of Average

By: *Yakinea Marie*

Right now take an assessment and look at your life; are you living at the level that you desire? Are your dreams becoming your reality daily? Be honest with yourself because self-evaluation is one of the great keys to growth and fulfillment. It shines the light on areas of weaknesses and strengths that you can intentionally work on or build upon. This is not possible if you neglect the personal assessment or evaluation period that's centered around your life. Self-evaluation is filled with many probing questions that one must ask themselves if they desire to live life beyond average. My success principle "Living

Outside The Box of Average" shines light on the BOX OF AVERAGE that many entrepreneurs and aspiring entrepreneurs are locked into simply by choice. Regardless of the excuse we may choose for abiding in the place called "average", the final decision is up to us. No one has power over you, like YOU

Think about it.....If you had a choice would you elect to live an average or ABOVE average life? Would you prefer to experience ordinary or EXTRAordinary results in your business? Would you rather be known as a person who lives a life of quiet desperation because you accepted the common versus the uncommon lifestyle. Is your goal to be like everyone else, fit into the crowd of average, or STAND OUT as a trailblazer and innovator who added their own creative touch to the world?

One of the threats to your purpose is when you accept a life of average as your new normal: average living, thinking, being, or doing. Average is one of the many enemies to success.

Dictionary.com defines average as typical, common, and ordinary. When I process the definition in everyday life, I assess it as being complacent, mundane, and void of excitement and risk. As an entrepreneur "AVERAGE" is the death to your vision's growth and business success. From a personal perspective I define average as playing smaller than you are and were created to be; allowing the opinions of people, feelings of inferiority, and low self-worth to prevent you from taking risks and expecting more. I'm speaking from personal experience, because this was definitely my story. For years I convinced myself that I was not good enough or that I didn't qualify. While I had the support of others along with positive feedback, I was my worst enemy. I was comfortable with living an average or below average life, therefore growing a business at an average level was normal for me until I started reading books and associating myself with movers and shakers in the business arena. My mindset began to change, which led to me taking greater risks and expecting greater results.

In 2012, eight months before going full-time in my first company, fear was a part of my DNA. In June of that year I decided to initiate the task of hosting my first business conference under Kingdom Entrepreneurs International, while making only $9 dollars an hour on my fulltime job. I had no connections or financial backing, yet I had a vision. The conference cost me close to ten thousand dollars of which I acquired mainly through the contributions of sponsors. Many of my peers viewed me as being a bold woman of faith and a go-getter. I knew deep within myself that I had more to offer, but because of my feelings of inferiority I didn't go after my vision 100%. From 2012 – 2014 I hosted approximately ten events. Although I celebrate those wins, I later realized after attending a training in California in 2014 that I was playing extremely small as an entrepreneur. I was leaving tens of thousands of dollars on the table because I did only enough to host the events, but not enough to monetize them into a profitable business. When I changed my mindset, my actions changed, which caused my revenue to increase dramatically within one year of me launching my next company, the I Am Woman Business Network™ in January 2015.

When you expect greatness, greatness has a way of finding you. Innovators, visionaries, and trailblazers are attracted to those in motion regardless if they are new or seasoned in business. Money alone doesn't make you live an EXTRAordnary life and build an ABOVE average business. Money is the bi-product of a visionary who believed in themselves in spite of fear or setbacks and who refused to settle for anything less than God's best. The decision is ultimately yours. DECIDE TO LIVE BEYOND AVERAGE because there is MORE awaiting your arrival.

Below are several **Entrepreneurial Keys for Success**:
- **Average is the death to your vision's growth and business success.** No one holds the keys to your success in life but you. The decision to expand starts with YOU.

- **Leaders are readers.** Make reading personal growth books a part of your daily routine.
- **Become a master in your field of business.** Study to stay relevant, it builds confidence in how you deliver results to your clients.
- **Surround yourself with visionaries, go-getters, and trailblazers.** It will ignite a fire in you to reject complacency and take bigger risk.
- **Do one thing every day that stretches you, that makes you uncomfortable.** That one thing could be you going after a contract that you think is larger than what your company can handle, making a phone call and asking to speak at a major conference in another state or country, or expanding your business into multiple areas. Be grateful but do not become complacent.
- **Become comfortable with being uncomfortable.** Live outside the box of average and normal.

- **Don't get stuck by past successes.** Celebrate your past successes, but only for a moment, but remember it's impossible to conquer the future focusing on the past.
- **Never allow the contradictory opinions of others to prevent you from pursuing and reaching your goals.** One of the greatest freedoms that you will ever experience is when you GET FREE of people's opinion of you.
- **Expect to live an EXTRAordinary life in every area.** The only limits that exist are the ones that you place on yourself.

Yakinea Marie's purpose and passion in life is to see entrepreneurs live enriched, purposeful, and prosperous lives, while living out their truth authentically. She is a speaker, certified business coach, #1 Bestselling author, and the Founder and CEO of the I Am Woman Business Network™, a business training and development company that support women entrepreneurs in increasing their clientele, visibility, and profits. She is also Executive Director of the I Am Woman Network Foundation, Inc., which mentors and cultivates the next generation of young entrepreneurs. Yakinea Marie, known to her clients as The Wealth Strategist™, specializes in supporting entrepreneurs in creating a CEO Game plan to build a solid business foundation and increase their bottom-line. As a Minister of the gospel she finds fulfillment in helping others create a life of fulfillment through the Word of God. Connect with Yakinea Marie at www.YakineaMarie.com or www.IAmWomanNetwork.com.

# Embracing Your Identity
## By: Curtis K. Richardson

Embracing your identity is the foundation to success. The lack of connection will lead to destruction. We are born in a world that feeds off anxiety and stress. Anxiety and stress are learnt behaviors and not conducive to your true potential. There is an inner brilliance placed in us all. Careful, it can be smothered by our surroundings. If we were to take a page from a newborn, they are in pure bliss in this phase of their lives. Even when they're upset, it's not in a sense of worry, this is how they communicate with us. On the other hand, their joy is undeniable, pure, and untainted. They haven't learned any of the common practices of their environment yet. Fear doesn't exist and faith is 100 percent action. They understand, one must crawl before falling and walk before talking. They have this built into their natural design. In short, a newborn is more equipped than we think. Keep in mind, this newborn has just left the Creator. "Before I formed you **in the womb** I knew you…" (Jeremiah 1:5, NKJV). A newborn understands who he or she is and acts accordingly. We tend to lose this brilliance in a flawed environment. There are negative habits adopted, conditions applied, and raw genius forgotten, but not lost.

Growing up around the mid-eighties and early nineties in Birmingham wasn't pretty. There were drugs and violence in my neighborhood. It appeared that hopelessness was freely given on every corner and every turn. Drug money was a fad and marketed as the American dream to a 12-year-old. The gangs were equivalent to the local boys club. The weekend was the highlight of our lives, so much so, we made songs about it (Living for the Weekend by The O'Jays). I love that song (as I laugh out loud). The flawed environment became the norm, taking a toll on my natural essence. In adapting to my surroundings, I indulged in senseless behavior. I thought I knew all there was to know. I was keeping it real, not knowing I was just fake as can be. Around the age of 16, I discreetly picked up an interest of reading, biblical theology and history. From time to time I was jokingly called "the philosopher" by some of my peers. I hadn't fully embraced the fundamental concept of my divine identity, until I read in the bible, Genesis 1:26 "Let Us make man in Our image, according to Our likeness..." at about 21-years old. This text changed my life. This was my pivot, wrapped in a nutshell defining who I am. At this point, I realized, I am the success I was looking for. When you realize you are created in God's image and likeness, you are unstoppable.

    Five years later, in 2001, I started my first full time company. The beginning was a challenge of course and exciting at the same time. I had no business sense, but you couldn't have told me this back then. You can be good at what you do, yet lack appropriate business skills. Every now and then, the two are intertwined. Although I did not have all of the business sense, it didn't stop me. I learned some hard and expensive lessons. I can truly say that embracing my identity helped me through this time. Fear wasn't an option, although it tried raising its head every now and then. I am constantly reminding myself, I was created in God's image and His likeness. Today, I'm still standing on this truth.

Now that you understand the value in capturing this brilliance that was created by God himself, you must make this practical in your everyday living. You will find that you are unique. You may seem strange to some and weird to some as you view life through the lenses of your identity. Every action step you take from now on will be a step of value. Words that you've once known all your life have now changed their meaning. Challenges and oppositions are now seen as strength. In summary, when the going gets tough, the tough in you gets going. This is your new philosophy; you are ready to build.

Let's build a new and improved you by practicing the following **Entrepreneurial Keys for Success**:

- **Be clear on what you want.** This step is very important. Define what you want and be clear about it. You will find that this new identity will accomplish everything you put your mind to.
- **Make sure your "why" is in alignment with your divinity.** I ran my business for about eight years before I adopted this concept. I was the typical business with a typical mission statement. I was in business to be the largest contractor in the southeastern part of the states. But of course, I didn't reach beyond my town in my city. Once my "why" changed to, I'm doing this to create opportunity for others, I witnessed a rapid growth. In a manner of two months, I went from a 2-man crew, counting myself, to a 60-man crew.
- **Learn your craft, then once learned, learn some more.** By now, you will find that success is quite simple and attainable. You should have had passion when you started, but most don't. However, at this phase it's needed. Because, this is where the time

and work comes in, the learning never stops and if there's no passion, you will stop.

- **Know where you're going.** Vision may seem like it's the tip of the iceberg, yet in reality, it's the root of your faith. Nature demonstrates this well. A seed already knows its kind before its maturity. Before we see and experience that beautiful soft red and white apple, it once was a hard brown and black seed. If you know who you are, you will know where you are going.

Curtis K. Richardson, is first and foremost a man of God. He doesn't move without God's guidance. Curtis is the father to three amazing daughters and married to his beautiful wife of 19 years. He has been an entrepreneur most of his life and Founded C&J Electrical in 2001, one of the most recognized electrical companies in its industry.

Curtis is community driven. He serves as President of The Birmingham Metro Black Chamber of Commerce. He also serves on the Board of the Alabama State Black Chamber of Commerce. Curtis was appointed by Governor Robert Bentley to the Small Business Commission in 2014 and recently re-appointed in 2017. Also, recognized as a 2017 Small Business Advocate finalist by the National Small Business Administration in Washington, D. C.

Curtis was featured in the Birmingham Times as one of the top – minority businesses in Birmingham. He's had several awards and nominations through his tenure: Employer's Recognition Awards, Nominated for

Small Business Awards, ICCC Alumni, and Small Business Finalist on a national level.

Curtis emulates the qualities of a leader by daily remaining persistent in his commitment to improve his local area and its citizens. He positively contributes to his hometown of Birmingham, which he is dedicated to progressing by participating in prominent projects, employment throughout the region, and mentoring. www.curtiskrichardson.com.

# From Start to Finish College Smart™
### By: Mona Lisa Morris

I've always tried to do things without seeking help. Out of necessity, I learned to be independent at a very young age. I've always felt like I could figure things out on my own and I carried this attribute over into my attempt at starting a business. Independence is a great characteristic to carry over into any aspect of life, but for me, it hindered my progress of getting my business started.

There are many things you can do on your own when starting a business, but you have to know when it's time to seek help. You may be considered an expert in the field **of** your business, but are you an expert **in** starting a business? We may have many skill sets and talents, but it takes a specific set of skills and knowledge to start a business successfully.

Starting a business is not a small task. It takes strategic preparation, planning, and action. There were many tasks I could complete without seeking help in starting my business, but I needed help with certain tasks. Often times we have connections to professionals that can provide the skills we need with free guidance and help, but sometimes you have to decide to pay someone for guidance and help.

In this age of DIY (Do It Yourself), search engines and YouTube can provide tutorials on any subject you can imagine. Some may ask, "Why would you pay someone to help you when you could figure out how to do it yourself"? YouTube and the Internet can provide you with a lot of information, but more than likely, they can't provide you with every detail of what you need to know about starting your business.

I launched my business, Finish College Smart™, with a successful ribbon cutting ceremony and reception on June 16, 2017. Most people would not know it took me nearly five years to get to this momentous occasion. I came up with this great idea for my business, but sat on it and allowed every excuse to keep me from getting it started. I finally came to the realization that I needed help!

My experience with starting a business has taught me a valuable lesson. I have carried this principle of "knowing when to seek help" into all aspects of my life. I've always had a level of independence and would rarely seek help when I needed it. I've learned when to seek help and how much better things can be when you get the right help! Yes, starting a business costs money and doing things on your own can save you money. However, YouTube and the Internet are not giving you custom-tailored assistance for your specific business. Paying someone to help you get your business started can help you avoid some costly mistakes and save you money.

We all know that time is a precious commodity and once it has passed, we can never get it back. I have also learned that time is money. I wasted a lot of time and as result, money. I was thinking I could get everything done on my own when I could have simply paid someone to help me get things done. I could have started Finish College Smart™ much sooner and started making money sooner!

After coming to the realization that I needed help, I decided to hire a business coach. I was starting a business coaching students and parents on how to Finish College Smart™ ("*Finish college on time or less; finish college with little or no debt*™"), but I realized I needed a coach to help me start this business. I had extensive knowledge about how to finish college smart, but I needed help setting up the foundation of the business. I also needed a strategic plan and help from someone that has been specifically trained in the industry of starting a business.

My business coach also provided me with continuous motivation and accountability. Let's face it, *#it happens! And, it happens all the time. Life for me has always been juggling work and family commitments. So many things would come up that would make me easily put aside my aspirations for starting my business. My business coach kept me on track with a focus on the finish line, even when unexpected things came up.

Next, I sought the help of a branding manager. I knew that building my brand and getting the message out about my business was essential to making it a success. I understood the principle that you can have the best business or product in the world, but if it is not properly packaged and promoted, it is useless.

My business coach and branding manager have played essential roles in helping me get my business started. They helped me simplify the process. They also filled in the gaps and helped me when I just didn't have the time or specific knowledge to get certain tasks done on my own.

I'm not saying that it is mandatory to get a business coach and/or a branding manager. Every business is different, and every entrepreneur is different. Your needs may be different from what I needed to start Finish College Smart™. For example, you may need to seek help from an attorney, a marketing expert, or a social media guru. Although, those were not an immediate need for me, it may be for your business. You should identify what you need help with and seek the help to get your business started.

Listed below are a few **Entrepreneurial Keys for Success** that helped me in my journey:

- Realize it is okay to self- educate to acquire a better understanding of what it is you would like to do. It helps to ease some of the anxiety.

- Don't allow procrastination to steal your dream.
- Know when to seek help and don't be afraid to ask for it.
- Hire Professionals that are subject matter experts in their field and that will hold you accountable.

**Meet the author of *From Start to Finish College Smart*™:**
Mona Lisa Morris is a Certified College Funding Specialist and Education Loan Analyst. She is the Founder and CEO of Finish College Smart™, a company committed to helping students *finish college on time or less, and finish college with little or no debt.*

Mona Lisa has a passion for helping students and families earn debt-free college degrees. She created Finish College Smart™ to empower and equip students and families with strategies, tools, and resources that will assist them with an affordable and successful college experience. Her chapter provides insight into how she overcame setbacks in getting Finish College Smart™ started.

In addition to her certification as a Certified College Funding Specialist and Education Loan Analyst, Mona Lisa holds licenses in nursing and insurance. She is a graduate of Excelsior College. After a rewarding 25-year career in the health and insurance industries, her focus today is to help address the growing problems students face, including low college graduation rates and increasing college debt. For more information visit www.FinishCollegeSmart.com.

# Childlike Faith
By: Mishondy Wright-Brown

*"For verily I say unto you, If ye have faith as a grain of mustard seed, ye shall say unto this mountain, Remove hence to yonder place; and it shall remove**; and nothing shall be impossible unto you**."* Matthew 17:20 (KJV).

Navigating through life is challenging, even for those who don't choose entrepreneurship. When I decided to embark on this entrepreneurial journey, I had no idea what I was in for. All I knew was that I had a vision that I felt so passionately about, it kept me awake at night. I also knew that in order to bring this vision to fruition, I needed to work hard and have faith.

Faith is something that many people know about and claim that they exercise. I often hear people saying, "I have faith that God will take care of it", but sometimes you don't see supporting evidence that the individual truly has the faith that they speak of.

When I received the vision for "Don't Touch Me!" in 2013, I was not sure where to begin. The vision was to raise awareness of child molestation. As a Director of Nursing, I was not sure how that vision fit into the life I was leading at that time. I was living comfortably and was totally unaware that God had more planned for my life. Quite naturally, fear set in. I thought to myself; what am I supposed to do? How am I going to make this work? Where is the funding for this organization coming from? Those were a few of the questions that immediately clouded my thought process as I tried to maneuver my way in the entrepreneurial space.

At the embryonic phase of my business, I was filled with all kinds of emotions. All of those initial fear driven questions can get into one's head to the point where they become a resounding cymbal. Then I remembered what had allowed me to make it this far. I remembered faith, and not just any faith, but it was childlike faith. I believed that God was going to intervene and provide for me within my business just as He had done in every impossible situation I had ever encountered. I didn't spend time contemplating how or when. I merely believed that God is always there and He always made provision for each vision that He placed in me.

Do you remember when you were a little child and your parents asked you what you wanted for Christmas? You would get all excited and you would sit down with paper and pencil in hand and created a wish list. You weren't concerned with your parents' financial situation or their ability to find what it was that you were asking for. You wrote those items down and you knew in your heart on Christmas morning that you would awaken to a wish that had come true. You did not worry. You did not ask your parents how they were going to do it and you certainly didn't ask them when they were going to do it. In your world, your expectation was that your parents would have all of your items from your wish list. Imagine when you believed it was coming from Santa! You believed that a man, whom you had never seen, was going to grant you all of your heart's desires. He was going to travel the world, in one night, and arrive at each child's house with their specific toys. You never let fear stop you from wishing. You never questioned *how* it was going to happen. You went on about your business knowing that everything was going to be as you hoped it would be on Christmas morning!

    In that respect, I took my child-like faith, and I began working on the startup of my business. When I needed to purchase things for the organization, I believed that the money was going to come to me. I knew that God was going to make a way, regardless of what it looked like naturally. When I needed volunteers to assist me in the various live functions I held and/or attended, I knew that God would send the right people, if I simply made myself available. I took my child-like faith and went into action. I depended on God for the execution of *His* vision and trusted Him to make everything that I needed available to me.

That being said, my entrepreneurial journey began. Every day I look to God for directives. Whenever fear tries to creep in and cause me to second-guess my purpose, I am reminded to "…ask and it shall be given you; seek, and ye shall find; knock, and it shall be opened for you." Matthew 7:7. I write out my Christmas wish list (goals/visions) and know that my Father will bring all of those things to fruition on Christmas Day!

As you embark on your entrepreneurial journey, I challenge you to trust God with the faith of a child. Your Father is more trustworthy than Santa and He is sure to supply you with the provision for His vision.

**Entrepreneurial Keys for Success**:

- Have the faith of a child. Believe that God will show up and provide in your business just like He has in previous situations.
- Never allow fear to stop you from dreaming.
- Take your child-like faith and put it into action.
- Trust God to make provision for the vision.
- Trust God with the faith of a child.

Mishondy Wright-Brown is a Wellness Coach and Advocate. She is the Founder of "Don't Touch Me!", an organization with a mission to increase awareness of child molestation through awareness, education, and empowerment. She is passionate about assisting people on how to navigate through their wellness journey and heal from childhood experiences.

Ms. Wright-Brown is also the Master Wellness Coach at Mishondy Wright Wellness, where she combines her own wellness practices with the practices of other wellness practitioners and helps others live a balanced life by achieving physical, mental, spiritual, emotional and financial wellness. She is a native of North Carolina, but makes the DC Metro area her home. You can find her on Facebook at: Mishondy Wright, RN Wellness Coach and on Instagram at: mishondywrightwellness.

# Fear

By: *Joe Lockett*

Fear can be your enemy or it can be your friend. I define fear as an unpleasant emotion caused by the belief that someone or something is dangerous, likely to cause a pain, or is a threat. A large number of entrepreneurs do not succeed because they fear success. Yes, you read that right! Take a minute and think about it. Have you experienced a six figure financial success or achieved the highest accolade for mastering a skill? Many people say they want to be financially successful; however, when it comes down to actually doing what it takes to be successful, people start to second guess themselves by over thinking and shortly afterwards, indecisiveness. When you start to find reasons why you don't have time to follow your dream right now, you have just experienced fear as defined above. Fear can be your friend by being the determining factor in some of your decision-making. I say this because fear puts you in the driver seat, forcing you to make choices on how to advance. There are decisions you must make when you are in the driver seat:

1. Put the keys in the ignition. Put the car in gear. See what happens.

2. Turn left. Turn right. Go forward. Go backward.

3. Or, get out of the car, and run away because you are afraid.

My wife was offered a lucrative position in another state. This put me in a position to reinvent myself by becoming flexible with the changes in our living situation. The profession I was in was not the right "game" to be in. After getting my wife settled in West Virginia, I laid on the bare floor (prior to the furniture arriving) for an entire day. Now, most of you can imagine your spouse looking at you crazy, with a mean side-eye, and becoming concerned about this sort of behavior. The next day, we went to dinner and I told my wife, "I'm going to do radio!" The look on her face was not the most pleasant. I had no answers to how I could pull this off. That day, I asked her to give me three years to grow and make a profit.

Faith in myself was the driving force and most important principle I could look to. I told my family about my decision to go into radio and become the next Steve Harvey. Syndication would be the ultimate goal. A family member said to me, "Everyone cannot be a Steve Harvey." And on the opposite side of the spectrum, another family member told me, "You can be anything you want to be. Put God first. I truly believe in you."

I was afraid because I had no idea how to get into radio. With only one person in my corner who believed I could do it, that gave me confidence to take the driver seat and put the keys in the ignition. I called my friend, Comedienne Joy, who was in radio during this time, and asked if I could come to one of the current shows to observe. The host was Hollis Wormsby, who said yes for me to shadow and watch his style of radio. Hollis said to me, "You just can't sit there and not say anything." He asked me to come to the microphone and tell his audience what I did for a living. I was nervous, but I spoke into the microphone and said my name is Joe Lockett and I am the DIY (Do It Yourself) expert for Fox 6 News. Later that week, Comedienne Joy called me and said Hollis wanted to know if I'd like to be part of their show as a DIY expert. I said yes and the following week I was on radio. I did that show for four months until it was cancelled. Fear set in again because I was back in the driver seat with no directions, but I acquired the knowledge of how to do radio. I asked Comedienne Joy and the other co-host on the show, Melva Tate, if they would be interested doing a radio show with me. They both, to my surprise, said yes! The Joe Lockett Show, "Love, Hate, and Debate" radio talk show on WYDE FM 101.1 FM was born.

I have faced many fears along my journey but now I don't view fear the same anymore. I see

God sending me a test to show me what I need to learn, understand, and to believe before he sends me my blessings.

Allow me to share a few **Entrepreneurial Keys for Success** and lessons from my journey and help you to face fear in a totally different manner:

- Look in the mirror and stop lying to yourself about what you know and what you don't know. The mirror does not lie. Write down the things you do not know. Go find people who know how to do the things on your list and ask for help.
- Go work for free to learn the skill you need.
- Friends and family will not see your vision; God gave it only to you.
- When you succeed, it's your fault.
- When you fail, it's your fault.
- Know what you want your business to look like when it grows up. For example, I wanted to have a radio show but I knew I wanted to syndicate the day God gave me the vision.

- Learn to face every fear head on. This will take time as some fears will be bigger than others. Just know, the sooner you face God's test, the sooner you will receive the blessing in it.
- If you have no fear, your goal is not big enough. God has something bigger waiting for you.
- Teach others along the way the secrets you use to face your fears. Pay it forward.

Joe Lockett is the Founder and CEO of The Joe Lockett Show, as well as the visionary behind JL Mentoring Camp and Joe's Lock & Learn program. The JL Show: TV - Alabama Cable network and radio WYDE 101.1 FM are news, entertainment and real talk about topics that matter to his audience. It's a radio and TV show for and about the people and the voices of the community no matter where that community lies.

Community First: The Joe Lockett philosophy would be nothing without giving back to the community. Joe's Lock & Learn program has given away over 4000 book bags over the last three years. In 2016 Joe created the JL Mentoring Camp for girls and boys, which served 30 families as a result of the free camp.

Joe has received numerous awards: the Who's Who in Birmingham, Men of Influence award, Mayor William A. Bell Sr. Small Business award, and William Robertson 2017 Entrepreneur of the Year Award. Joe is married to Michelle Lockett and have three beautiful children. To connect with Joe Lockett visit www.jlockettshow.com.

# Build Your Team & Circle The Wagons!

### By: Melva Tate

It is time to circle the wagons!!!

I vividly remember hearing my mother use this term while talking to her sisters in their attempt to handle an urgent family situation. Although I didn't understand the meaning, I knew they meant business and something serious was about to go down.

Since that time, I've used the term often. Sick family member – circle the wagons. Business crisis – circle the wagons. Disobedient children – circle the wagons!!!

The call to "Circle the Wagons" means it is time to unite for a common interest. It's time to come together in preparation for or to respond to an attack. The circling ensured that all hearts and minds assembled immediately to focus on the problem at hand.

As I grew my business, it became ever more important to have the right team around me because "circling" from time to time would be a necessity.

Teams are the lifeline of your business. They're the uniquely assembled group that helps you, the owner and visionary, move your mission forward. Collectively, they have (or should have) the same mindset and attitude towards assisting your clients, selling your products, or serving as your brand ambassador.

Anyone who knows me or has spent time with me during Football Season, knows that I'm a football fanatic, a real fanatic. I take the "fan" thing to another level: high school, college, (mainly the SEC) and the NFL. Any given Friday, Saturday, or Sunday from August through January, you will find me in the stands or in front of the television cheering on my favorite team.

It's more than the action on the football field that keeps me attentive. I remain transfixed on teams and the way they function, if effectively, like a well-oiled engine. All of the moving parts excite me - some small, some large, some odd shapes and sizes, all working in harmony to achieve a common goal.

On the football field the players all seem to have the same tenacity, the same drive, and the same perseverance to get the job done. Teams in business should have that same drive and dedication. So, consider yourself the coach, committed to building a championship team, one player at a time. Teams unite against the opponent. Teams work in unison. Teams circle the wagon.

I don't remember the exact day. But, I remember the feeling. I was tired. I was drained. I was exhausted. And to top it off, I had reverted to working for minimum wage. Well not really minimum wage, but the hours I put in to manage and grow my business sure felt that way. I had just celebrated my fifth-year anniversary running my Human Resource Management/Career Development consulting firm. And I was doing it all by myself. I was serving clients, submitting proposals, training employees facilitating workshops, handling social media. ALL OF THE ABOVE. I had turned my passion and purpose into a problem.

I questioned if this coaching and consulting thing was really for me or if I should run back to the comfort of a six-figure salary with all the great perks, including the company car and credit card. It was not until I hit my breaking point that I realized although I had the skills to do it all, I was not effective. The sheer magnitude of work products and demands of my time made it nearly impossible to do this business thing alone.

After convincing myself that I needed to share the load, the first question was how could I afford to do so. Yea – that money thing always comes into play. I stepped back and sternly told myself – how can you NOT afford to? If I continued to miss client deliverables, was stressed to the max, and challenging my purpose, eventually there would be no business. It was time to circle the wagons!

As I reflect on my team building challenges, it frustrated me that a mouthpiece that preaches the importance of teams, tried to function without one. I was trying to function "Solo" that I didn't realize I was functioning "so low." Listen and hear me clearly on this – You need a team. Don't wait until you're questioning your purpose. Start building your team now.

My 'put in the work' **Entrepreneurial Keys for Success** and principles for building your team, one player at a time, are pretty simple.

- Be clear about your mission – who and how you serve. If you are confused, your team will be too.
- Document your processes. Your team will need clear guidance, play by play.
- Make a list of things that are important AND impactful for your business.
- Determine what important function can be delegated without impacting how you serve.
- Recruit for the skill-set(s) needed to be effective. Don't just select someone that fits the criteria to work under budget!
- Interview well. Make sure every member is a positive addition to the team versus a negative addition, which will add more stress to you.
- Hire slow, evaluate performance, and fire fast (and in that order).
- Commit to making the team member better than when they initially joined you.

- Treat your team members with dignity and respect. They joined the team to take the load off of you.
- Get out of their way and let them do the job. Accountability is important, but certainly don't micromanage.
- Realize teammates will move on. They are on your team for a reason, season or lifetime. Maximize the time you have with them.
- Repeat the process until your team is fully assembled.

My monthly calendar is filled with appointments to work with leaders across the US to select, manage and train their teams. Some function like the University of Alabama's championship football team (Roll Tide) and others like the Bad News Bears. Honestly, there are days that my own team resembles both. Do you know what we do during those challenging times when there is a breakdown in team dynamics? Yes – you guessed it. We circle the wagons……………..

**Melva Tate** lives by one rule: "**Put in the work.**" She also recruits, coaches and owns an award-winning business according to the "**PITW**" rule.

Melva has been putting in the work for more than two decades, serving as the Director of HR & Administration for two start-up organizations, before launching her own company. She's a radio personality, best-selling author, and a feature writer and contributor to leading newspapers and magazines.

In 2008, Melva followed her dream and launched Tate & Associates, LLC. She manages three unique divisions: ***Strategic HR Partnerships***, ***Career Touchdown and Melva Tate Speaks.*** The firm specializes in executive talent searches, human resource consulting, training and development, and career coaching to businesses, universities and nonprofit organizations.

Putting in the work like this leads to an impressive list of credentials, including a B.S. degree in Human Resource Management, an Executive MBA, Certified Life Coach and Professional in Human Resources certifications.

While Melva's official title is Human Capital Strategist, she's best described as a networking master and high-energy coach. Her passion is seeing people and companies flourish, and she is driven to nurture dreams and cultivate relationships. While paying clients keep the lights on, Melva also accepts the currency of handshakes, hugs, and Facebook friend requests. You can find her on social media platforms engaging her connections as The Career Coach. Learn more at www.MelvaTate.com.

I Said, "YES"

I AM
DETERMINED

# Kissing Your Excuses Goodbye

By: Mary Sood

By the age of ten, I had literary ambitions, an entrepreneurial spirit, and a yearning to see the world. There was no question that I would one day walk in the trifold vision God gave me. One day, I would write fiction, own a business, and traverse the globe. One day I would live boldly, beautifully and fully.

"If you can dream it, you can do it" was my mantra. This quote, printed on a poster of a ballerina I hung on my dormitory wall over 30 years ago, resonated so deeply that I felt as though Walt Disney had written it just for me.

In my sophomore year of college, my entrepreneurial zeal exploded when someone handed me an Avon catalogue. I immediately signed up to be a salesperson and began chasing students across the campus trying to convince them to wear more lipstick. Eventually my friends reminded me that they only had two lips, didn't want thirty shades of lipstick, were as broke as I was, and needed me to stop harassing them about buying cosmetics.

After college, I began a promising career as a public relations director. I had the honor of meeting and being photographed with people like the late Harold Washington, Chicago's first African American mayor. I still had my literary ambitions, my entrepreneurial spirit and my passion for travel. I also had a plethora of excuses for not finding time to write fiction. I was busy writing news releases all day, I told myself. Besides, the one literary agent who was interested in my work suggested so many drastic changes to a novel draft I submitted that I would have had to quit my job to complete the suggested edits. Forget the entrepreneurial plans; wasn't I lucky to land a job as a PR director when I was only in my mid-twenties? Besides, one of my goals was to travel and I was traveling frequently - fulfilling one out of three goals wasn't so bad, *right?*

I had so many excuses for not living as I intended to live that if I stacked all of my excuses in a pile, I could have built a stairwell to the top of the Sears Tower. Yet, I felt as though I had a common bond with every entrepreneur I met, whether it was the late John Johnson, who founded Ebony Magazine, or someone hawking gold-plated chains at a busy intersection. They were entrepreneurs and I was an entrepreneur in my mind. Ditto for fiction writers. I hung out in libraries and perfected the art of living vicariously.

After I married, I moved to smaller and smaller cities where opportunities seemed increasingly scarce. When I became a mother, I had an even grander pile of excuses for not walking in my vision: diapers, play dates, and endless doctor's appointments.

But motherhood also brought me face to face with the question, "What legacy do I want to leave?" I wanted to teach my children to live boldly, beautifully and fully. So I wrote a couple of books and started a publishing company. In those days, there was no Amazon Createspace to print, package, sell and ship products. I had to do everything myself. It was demanding, but I was thrilled to exercise my entrepreneurial muscle.

Time brought more opportunities. Like many children, my kids tended to slouch at the table. I reminded them of their table manners so often that I thought, "I could start an etiquette business." So I did. I studied the industry; invested in beautiful tableware; and convinced the manager of a bookstore to let me teach classes in their back room. I kept the business for several years, but when a new manager chose to use the back room to store discounted books, I had to find a new venue.

None of the new locations worked. If one class session was packed, the next two would be almost empty. Just when I figured there was no need to renew my business license, a physician's office asked me to present a business etiquette workshop for their staff. I flung myself into that project. This opportunity led to a couple of out-of-town opportunities. One day, after conducting a workshop at a conference in Memphis, I pulled up to a McDonald's to buy a hamburger. My car stopped without any sign of a warning. Although I was ready to take my show on the road, my car was ready for a leisurely life that precluded out of town business trips. Later, I began conducting training workshops for an international company. It was a phenomenal opportunity. Unfortunately, the company ownership changed and requests for my services waned.

Finally, I did what many discouraged entrepreneurs do. I gave up and found a part-time job that allowed me to earn a steady paycheck while raising my children. Fortunately, several years later, when I finally decided to kiss my excuses goodbye, I came home to the dreams God placed in my heart decades ago.

I became a PR consultant and also launched a new publishing company, Mom 'N' I Publishing, LLC, which produces books that educate, inspire and motivate readers. I also began writing fiction and had a story published in a literary magazine. Although I was already a seasoned traveler, I learned to say yes to even more exciting travel opportunities. Occasionally I think, "What if I had not abandoned the businesses I started years ago?" or "What if I hadn't taken such a long hiatus from writing fiction?" I don't ask these questions for myself because I think that any time you let go of excuses and begin living the life you were meant to live, you deserve to celebrate without regrets. I ask these questions for the sake of younger people who might read my words. Any time is a good time to begin living boldly, beautifully and fully. But the sooner you kiss your excuses goodbye, the sooner you will begin walking in your vision.

**Entrepreneurial Keys for Success**:
- Kiss your excuses goodbye and live life boldly, beautifully and fully.
- Celebrate without regret and start where you are.
- Never give up on your dreams.
- Never be afraid to take a risk.

Mary Sood is an award-winning publisher, communications professional, speaker and author. She has utilized her expertise in public relations to help academic, corporate and non-profit organizations and entities enhance their brand perception. She has provided services to Delta Gastroenterology, The McNealey Group, Stillman College, Jackson State University, Rally's Hamburgers, Jack and Jill of America, the American Cancer Society, AARP, the Jackson Madison County Library and others.

Sood is the co-owner of Mom 'N' I Publishing, LLC, which produces educational and inspirational books for all ages. Sood's writing has been featured in the *Birmingham Arts Journal, Stillman Magazine* and other publications. She has been featured on radio and television, most recently appearing on *Talk of Alabama* on Birmingham's ABC 33/40. She holds a Master of Arts in Romance Languages from the University of Memphis and a Bachelor of Arts from the University of Wisconsin-Eau Claire. She sponsors the annual Mom 'N' I Publishing/American Advertising Federation-Tuscaloosa Diversity Scholarship and various competitions to encourage success. Books by Mom 'N' I Publishing, LLC include *Freshman Fifteen: The Most Important Things I Learned in My First Year of College* and *Yellow Kitten Learns Good Manners.*

For additional information and to connect visit www.momnipublishing.com.

# Consistency

By: *Jakim L. Jackson*

There are several success habits that a person must have in order to accomplish his or her goals. Consistency is one of those very important keys. It is the driving force behind achieving your goals. Consistency is defined as having steadfast adherence to the same principles, course, form, or task and doesn't vary greatly in quality over time. Based on this definition this can be an asset or liability for you. "Why is this", you may ask? You may feel that because you're consistent at something you should be good, right? That isn't always the case. You can actually be consistent in areas that are not beneficial to you.

As an entrepreneur I've learned that first you need to identify what you want out of life and what you want to accomplish. Next you want to write a step-by-step plan on how you're going to get there. Have goals set in place throughout your plan to help push you toward reaching them. Now, you're set. By following these steps you'll know what to constantly devote your time to. Remember, in order to reach your goals, you will have to recognize what is or isn't a distraction. Anything pulling you away from your goals or slowing you down from accomplishing them, eliminate it. Become laser focused, have tunnel vision towards fulfilling your destiny, because it's yours.

The moment you lose sight of your goals, you put yourself in jeopardy of falling off track. This can result in becoming consistent in the wrong areas, doing things that stunt your growth, or that pull you away from your destiny. So you see, consistency is a very important habit to develop and maintain. Now ask yourself this question; is what I'm doing daily consistently helping or hurting me? Are my daily activities pulling me closer to reaching my goals or pushing me out of sight of them? We are creatures of habit, and if we continue the same routine on a continuous basis, the results will reflect just what it is that we have made a habit.

Make what you're doing count for something. Consistency requires that you do something repetitively. You can't do it one or two times and expect to do something great. Nothing happens overnight, there is always a preparation period. Be patient, be consistent, and put in the work. That was something I had to learn myself first hand. Wanting and wanting, talking and talking, but not putting in the consistent work to reach the goals I set out to achieve. It was a repetitive cycle. I'm sure some of you can attest to this. Working on something for a day then stopping for three months will yield no results. You will find yourself back at square one every time.

It can become quite frustrating. One thing that God has blessed us with, is time. There is no need to worry or beat yourself up. Get up, push harder, and give it another try, because nothing can beat failure like trying again. Don't waste valuable time and energy by only putting in the work every once in a while. If you want something bad enough and you feel it's in your heart to accomplish it, then put in the work. You can't just sit back and talk about what you're going to do and only watch Netflix with your spouse. Talking about what I was going to do was my main problem. If you're sitting back wasting time, chilling, and talking about how you're "going to do it", there is someone out there executing. They are putting in the consistent work and allowing their results to do the talking for them. So I challenge you friend, stop talking about it and start doing. Although we're blessed with time, it's a gift, it goes by quickly and we never know how much time we actually have. Live life to the fullest. Try and enjoy every second of every day. Put in the work, remain consistent, keep God first, and soon success will be in your grasp.

**Entrepreneurial Keys for Success**:
- Consistency is the driving force behind achieving your goals.

- Identify what you want out of life and what you want to accomplish.
- Write a step-by-step plan on how you're going to achieve your goals.
- Have goals set in place throughout your plan to help push you toward reaching them.
- Make God a priority in building your business.

Jakim L. Jackson, a native of Birmingham, AL, has a passion for entrepreneurship and real estate. He's had the honor of serving in the Marine Corp shortly after graduating high school. Jakim is currently the manager for Rutledge Properties. He is married with 3 beautiful children. Connect with Jakim on Facebook at Jakim L. Jackson.

## Stay Within Your Gifts and Talents

By: SL Stoutermire

When you set out to become an entrepreneur, it's wise to stay within your gifts and talents. When I first started out, it wasn't easy, because I didn't focus on my gifts and talents. I became discouraged. I almost gave up several times. I want to help you avoid a mistake I made as I ventured out to become an entrepreneur. I had to learn that I wasn't meant to do everything. I was created to do specific things that aligned with my gifts and talents. This is where I would find my greatest peace and joy as an individual as well as an entrepreneur.

You may be asking yourself, "What is my gift and what is my talent?".

A gift can be defined as the following:
- a notable capacity, talent, or endowment
- a special ability for doing something
- A G<u>ift</u> often implies special favor by God or nature.

A talent can be defined as the following:
- special often athletic, creative, or artistic aptitude
- general intelligence or mental power; <u>ability</u>
- the natural endowments of a person
- a special ability that allows someone to do something well
- T<u>alent</u> suggests a marked natural ability that needs to be developed.

When you apply these two words to entrepreneurship, it simply means understanding and knowing what you are called to do and doing those things that come natural to you. If you are horrible at painting, you wouldn't become an artist.

Yet if you are a great mathematician, you may decide to become an accountant.

I have some questions for you as an entrepreneur. Are you staying within your gifts and talents? Are you operating within the area you are truly called to operate in? Are you doing the thing(s) that drive you to get up in the morning with so much passion and excitement that you can't stop focusing on it? Don't take on someone else's dream or vision if it doesn't align with your gift or talent.

I was afraid and nervous when I decided I wanted to become an entrepreneur. I initially discussed it with my husband and my inner circle. Everyone was excited and supportive. Everyone had ideas about what I should do. That became a serious issue. I was so eager to set out on my own that I listened to every idea and I tried to do them. I became frustrated and tired. I felt a great sense of dissatisfaction with everything I was doing. I was angry that it wasn't all falling in place. I didn't want to hear any more suggestions from people because they were only "suggesting" not helping. I eventually stopped exploring the idea of entrepreneurship and decided to go back into the traditional workplace.

I started job hunting but I couldn't find the "right" job. I couldn't find the job that would allow me to do what I was really great at doing. That's when it hit me!! All of this time, I was focused on doing what other people thought I should be doing and not what I knew I should be doing. I needed to focus on my gifts and talents. I had to go back to the reason why I was driven to become an entrepreneur.

I created a gifts and talents board. I listed all of my gifts and talents and what I wanted to do as an entrepreneur. I used it to define my vision as an entrepreneur and how my gifts and talents aligned with my vision. I ranked my ideas, gifts and talents from most exciting to least exciting. From this, I was able to see how I could intertwine them to create my overall vision. Next, I drew my vision. I needed to know what it would look like so I could make adjustments. Then, I wrote my mission for my vision by looking back at everything that reflected what I saw in my mind and felt in my heart. I revamped it until it reflected the entrepreneur that I was meant to be in life. I researched my vision, wrote a business plan and set goals and timelines to remain on course. I challenged myself to work harder when I became weary or stuck. There were times when I had to clear my mind and refresh myself. CAUTION! Don't get so overwhelmed that you start to resent the work you are doing to get your business started.

When people made suggestions, I reminded myself that they had my best interest at heart but they didn't know my heart's interests. I'm challenging you to go back and look at your vision as an entrepreneur. Ensure that it's centered around your gifts and talents. Storms will occur but the sun will shine again and it will be even brighter than before the storm occurred. The storms don't seem as bad when you are doing what you love.

Remember you are your greatest asset. No one understands you better than YOU. Don't give up. Allow yourself the freedom to do what you love and love what you do. It truly is the greatest sense of the fulfillment. If it doesn't make you want to leap out of bed to do it or not go to sleep because you're still working on it, then you may want to revisit your vision. Everyone won't understand your decisions or process. That's okay because it's your process, not theirs. It wasn't meant for them to understand.

If I had to do it all again, I wouldn't change anything. I learned and gained more than I lost in the end. I'm able to help other entrepreneurs not endure the same issues. What do you truly desire to do as an entrepreneur? Does it align with your natural gifts and talents? If not, is it possible for it to align with your gifts and talents?

"The artist is nothing without the gift, but the gift is nothing without the work." -Emile Zola-

**Entrepreneurial Keys for Success**:
- Remember that you are your greatest asset.
- Allow yourself the freedom to do what you love.

- Make sure that your vision is centered around your gifts and talents.
- Challenge yourself to work harder when you become weary or stuck and don't be afraid to take the time to clear your mind and refresh yourself.
- Don't take on someone else's dream or vision if it doesn't align with your gift or talent.

SL Stoutermire, is the Founder and CEO of SL Stoutermire, LLC. She is a wife, mother, author, speaker, advocate, voice for the voiceless, business owner, and Ambassador for God.

As an author SL Stoutermire's books are to inspire and empower. She encourages individuals not to lose faith because they can overcome their circumstances. Her books also will encourage readers to follow the path that God has them on and to trust the Holy Spirit to guide them.

SL Stoutermire has received several awards. Among the awards she's received is the Certificate of Merit Award, awarded by President Barack Obama and the American Red Cross. She's also been awarded and recognized as an American Graduate Champion in the Community. She's received a Commendation from the Governor of the State of Alabama and a Proclamation from the Mayor and City Council of Vestavia Hills. She has served and continues to serve on boards and committees throughout the State of Alabama. SL Stoutermire is a writer for an Alabama Publication.

She is the author of the international bestseller **"Strength, It's What I Found When I Removed My Makeup"**. She's currently working on three, soon to release, books.

To learn more about SL Stoutermire visit www.slstoutermire.com.

# Resilience

By: *Linda H. Lee*

Resilience is something I have observed strongly in children. Not to exclude other age groups, however, children have proven themselves to be strong. Children can grow up in poverty, be removed from their homes, have their life shattered by some type of catastrophe, experience a health altering experience, yet they still manage to be resilient. In the respect of resilience, I have studied and emulated my life after someone that as a child was raped at the age of nine, molested by two family members at the age of ten, by 14, she was pregnant and managed to keep it a secret until the baby was born. Tragically, she endured the death of her premature baby. This child has grown up to be the awesome queen of talk, owns her own television network, is a philanthropist, and has the highest net worth of any African American at the time of this writing. She is none other than the magnificent Oprah Winfrey.

Oprah embodies mental toughness and has bounced back regardless of many setbacks. Resilience is the capacity to recover quickly from difficulties; having toughness. Resilience also means to have the ability to recover from or adjust easily to misfortune or change; and the ability to recover readily from illness, depression, adversity, or the like.

I have many titles. Some of them are wife, mother, author, minister, life and relationship strategist, Marriage and Family Therapist (MFT), and entrepreneur. But before I gained any of those titles and roles, I too, have faced several setbacks in my quest to becoming self-employed. One experience that stands out the most, is when I decided to go back to school to obtain my master's degree in Human Development and Family Studies.

I was working a full-time job, a wife and mother of three teenagers and one of them at that time was faced with serious physical and health related issues. One challenge was that I wasn't as smart as I thought I needed to be to attain a master's degree. I didn't pass the entry exam, but I had good grades. As a result I was allowed into the master's program. After four years, I joyfully received my master's degree, which took others only two years to complete. It did not matter how long I had to attend school I was determined to finish. This was a major accomplishment for me.

Now, I am on my way to becoming a licensed MFT. NEWSFLASH: there is a hurdle I need to get over. I need to pass the state board licensing examination. Oh, that should not be a problem at all since I had acquired my degree. Surely, I can pass this exam, so I thought. After ten failed attempts, thousands of dollars spent on study materials and many defeating thoughts; I sought advice from people in my field of expertise as to what I should do. I was advised to continue to use my gift to counsel and provide advice to others by other avenues. I was advised to become a life coach, write a book or books, be a speaker, etc.. Subsequently, I decided to take their advice and become a life coach, which I renamed life and relationship strategist to be more specific.

Needless to say, I felt like I was a failure when I did not pass the state board exam. Especially, when I would miss the required score by three or four points sometimes. That setback took the wind out of my sail. I was defeated in spirit, mind and body. I didn't want to do anything but sit back and receive my retirement check every month from the State of Alabama for 25 years of service. Although I was working with two other networking companies and making money from speaking engagements, I knew that I could create wealth by other less stressful means. For me, that was my gift to advise and teach people on life and relationship issues. After hiring a business coach and enrolling in an online entrepreneur 6 weeks course I realized that I was my greatest commodity and asset. I am on my way to becoming one of the highest paid speakers and most sought out life coaches ever.

That is what I tell myself everyday. When you are resilient you begin to believe that anything is possible.

**Entrepreneurial Keys for Success** that helped me in my journey:
- Never give up. After ten attempts of not passing my MFT license exam, didn't mean that I could not perform what I was educated and gifted to do.
- Be innovative. Look for other possibilities and options.
- Seek counsel from others. In the multitude of counsel there is safety and provision.
- Research other entrepreneurs that have experienced life challenges and setbacks, yet resilient.
- Remember that a setback is waiting on the opportunity to make a comeback.
- You have the power within you to create whatever future you want.
- Continuous Education is necessary.

Linda H. Lee is self-employed as a Marriage and Family Therapist and Life and Relationship Strategist. She is also a minister, author, inspirational speaker and television producer. She received her Master Degree from The University of Alabama in Human Development and Family Studies and her Bachelor Degree in Business Administration and Organizational Management from Stillman College Management Institute.

    Linda is the Founder of "Strong Women Armed Together" (S.W.A.T.), which started in 1999. S.W.A.T. focuses on helping women find and fulfill their God given purpose.

    In 2004 Linda produced and hosted a show called "Issues of Life" that aired on Tuscaloosa local television station and surrounding counties for two years that dealt with the everyday issues of life. She also created and taught a bible study for Stillman College students called "Hour of Power", and in 2005 she conducted a bible study geared toward women issues that was held at Hannah Home for battered and abused Women. Currently, conducting meetings at a local facility in Albert City.

She has been featured in Tuscaloosa Magazine Fall 2004 issues as one of six most intriguing people. The article described her as a spiritual healer. She was also covered in The Net Work Directory 2005. Connect at www.LindaHLee.com / email: contact@LindaHLee.com.

## Trust the Process
### By: Ferlando Parker Sr.

Trusting the process is like growing a garden. You have to plant seed and trust the fact that they'll grow into what you need them to be. This is great analogy to starting a business. There are certain things you have to do. You have to first plough the field, then plant the seeds, and afterward allow it time to grow.

For example, my son and I are working on a remote control solution for customers. Most of our customers have multiple remote controls and after we install their television, many of them ask whether or not they will have to use different remotes to control their television. In an effort to support them I've been thinking of ways that we can provide a solution to this challenge. I am extremely busy and because of this I can't take on any additional responsibilities, but I knew I could find a solution by planting the seed and idea into my son. By planting that seed it is leading him toward trusting the process of learning the business and knowing how to provide the service. Thereafter, it will grow. Going through the process will lead to us being known statewide for that added service of programing remote controls which, in turn, will provide convenience and value to our customers.

How do I get my business there, you may ask? You have to start with people who are dedicated. Then, you have to plant seed through marketing. When growing a new business or introducing a new product, the question that you must ask is how are you going to market it? Keep in mind, you may not make a profit until your volume increases, allowing you to surpass the break-even point.

In the previous example of my son learning the remote control, he spent approximately ten hours working on it over the course of two months. His initial level of commitment wasn't enthusiastic, but he is now taking it serious. After working on it with us he realized the potential and the money that we could make by providing alternatives to programming remote controls by using new apps on the customer's phones.

As a result, the process is learning the solution and building marketing channels that will attract your targeted customer. Trusting the process is trusting that this will generate revenue. For example, if this was the only service we provided, this would be a startup company, just getting things off the ground. As the owner of a business you must trust the process to get it off the ground. Many times people refuse to trust the process because they want something from the onset (the beginning phase of the business). Some still hold onto their jobs while trying to straddle the fence of building a business. It doesn't always work out well because they're not able to dedicate themselves wholeheartedly to the business that they would like to have. It's like a relationship or marriage: if you're not building it with a lot of trust, it will not work.

When I first began hanging televisions, people didn't understand how it would work. It was hard to explain to people how it would work, but I had to trust the process. With my business ihangTVs.com, I also had to trust the process when hiring employees because you can hire the wrong people. If you're not careful your employees can have you in a position of feeling like what you're doing is not working. As the business owner there are several things that you must know: who your target customers are, what their immediate needs are, and what makes them happy. You also must know what makes you money. Hiring the wrong people may discourage you. If you have added the wrong person or people to your team, it can be a letdown to you if they are not able to replicate what you're doing or provide the level of service you are determined to provide.

**Entrepreneurial Keys for Success**:
- Understand that not all businesses immediately make money.
- Most businesses fail in 3-5 years if not operated correctly.
- Develop discipline early, especially with your earnings. It's like farming. If you don't work, you don't eat. I started with zero. With my first $250, I used forty percent of it and bought business cards, fliers, and marked coroplast signs to hang on telephone poles. I did whatever was necessary to make my phones ring. I kept doing it that way for three years before I opened my first office. In managing and distributing my company's revenue I use the 30-40-30 process: 30% goes to me, 40% goes toward operations and overheard, and 30% goes toward labor.
- Separate your personal and business transactions.
- If you're going to have a business or concept, you have to have a plan to get there.
- Develop the 3 feet rule. Everyone within three feet of me knows what my business is.
- There are no excuses.

Ferlando Parker Sr., Founder and CEO of ihangTVs.com, an audio video and data company, provides home and business audio video entertainment, along with convenience, to customers in the Southeastern region.

      Ferlando is an advocate for youth and young adults. Through various mentoring programs and growth opportunities Ferlando provides a forum that encourages, develops, and trains young males to be productive citizens in society. Ferlando has received numerous awards, one being the Birmingham Award for 5 consecutive years for best in business in audio video. For additional information and to connect with Ferlando Parker Sr. visit www.ihangTVs.com.

# I Said, "YES"

## I AM DESTINED FOR GREATNESS

# From Ministry to the Marketplace

By: Juarkena Pitts

Making the decision to monetize your gifts and talents can be very difficult in any normal or secular capacity. The idea of taking those gifts and talents to the marketplace in a fee for service business can be hard to conceptualize, as well as hard to execute, especially if you are like me. I was born and raised in the church with the expectation that you are to give anything and everything to God with no hesitation, no reservation, and no expectation of compensation. This line of faulty thinking is the disease and paralysis that plagues and contends with so many gifted entrepreneurs within the church. Without being pious, from my understanding, all of the disciples were successful businessmen prior to walking in ministry! The Bible says in 3 John 2, " I wish above all things that you prosper and be in good health, even as your souls prospers." The plan for our lives includes the wonderful gift of prosperity!

Most members of the church who consider themselves active and faithful in service have a heart for the Lord and his people and are willing to serve in various capacities. Often times, it is in the service of the ministry that one finds their purpose, their calling, and those special areas they have been gifted in. For one, it may be the gift of interior design that they discover while decorating for various events and services. For another, it may be writing and journalism they discover while managing the church blog and newsletter. In any case, the discovery has ignited a new sense of purpose and the resulting passion unlocks doors and streams of revenue not previously available or considered.

Central principles to the heart of the entrepreneur are always, creating revenue streams and reinventing oneself. These principles require investment in order to be developed, cultivated, and enlarged. For the entrepreneur who is looking to leave their salaried position in corporate America, this requires additional resources of time: often after hours, late nights, early mornings and weekend detail. The investment of coaching and training may be necessary. The entrepreneur may have the best idea for a product or service, but a business coach may be required to help them launch and move out of analysis paralysis – meaning you analyze something so much and for so long that you remain stuck in the analysis stage. Aside from the investment of time, coaching, and training, is always the investment of money. Money is necessary to research, market, create, design, and craft your product or service. The entrepreneur must understand this principle: ***Everything of value requires investment and costs resources to create that value.***

Understanding that principle has helped to frame my thinking any time I am hired to provide a service. This is especially true with regard to those with whom I serve and worship. This principle has become my foundation when discussing the scope of services my husband and I provide through our business enterprise. For our church, we happily facilitate many of our public relations functions and needs as well as provide consulting on major projects that require technology, public relations aspects, and publishing. As a unit, we decided that this is our reasonable and rational service to God accordingly to Romans 12:1 "I beseech you therefore, brethren, by the mercies of God, that you present your bodies a living sacrifice, holy, acceptable to God, *which is* your reasonable service." Nevertheless, we, along with all entrepreneurs in the church, must separate our service *to* the church from those whom we may serve *in* the church. We are clear and unapologetic about the resources required to provide our services and products. Moreover, we communicate the investment required to obtain them.

Remember, your products have value. Your ideas have value. Your time has value. Your training has value. According to Luke 10:7, the laborer is worthy of his hire. You are entitled to be compensated for a service or product you have been hired to provide. Ultimately, once you are able to quantify and understand the value of the resources you invest for your business, others will invest in that value and you will be successful in the marketplace.

Tips for Practical Application and **Entrepreneurial Keys for Success**:

- **Pray**. The decision to start a business when your understanding of "serving" has been limited can be difficult. Prayer and hearing God's perfect plan for me has always settled any doubts and fears. I encourage you to do the same to be led of the Lord.
- **Be delivered from people.** Whether it is in the church or outside of the church, someone will always have something to say about what you're doing or not doing. You must be free and confident in yourself to not

care what people think. If you allow people to control your thoughts and actions, you will never achieve the greatness and prosperity promised to you.
- **Set clear boundaries.** Be upfront and clear about what you consider serving in the course of ministry is and what requires an investment. Do yourself a favor and be sure to not muddy your own waters. Keep your business and business deals off of church grounds unless you are engaged by your church otherwise.
- **Be honest and transparent.** If you want to be paid, make that clear. Establish any payment requirements prior to beginning any project or service.
- **Learn to say "no".** If what you're being asked to do disturbs your peace, say "no". If you are not willing to give your products and services away, then don't, and feel confident about making that decision. **Do what keeps you at peace. Apply the "set clear boundaries" above.**

- **See your own value.** If you do not see the value in what you're doing, the service you are providing, or the product you're launching, no one else will. You must believe in yourself above all others. Consumers respect that confidence and they will invest in you or your product if you can deliver that to them.

**Juarkena Pitts**, the *Executive Life Empowerment Strategist* ™, is a Certified Master Executive Life Leadership Coach, Best Selling Author, Industry Leader, Keynote Speaker, Dynamic Teacher, and Licensed Minister who synergizes her experience and training, seasoned with wisdom, grace and transparency to catapult her clients and audience into destiny.

**Juarkena**, is the founder of Purposed to Empower©, a business designed to empower individuals and corporations. Purposed to Empower offers training and education programs through coaching, consulting, advising and mentoring, as well as, personal, business, and leadership training and development. **Juarkena** is also the co-founder and Chief Operations Officer of Greater Works Enterprises, LLC, a business conglomerate offering services specializing in publishing, graphic design, and small business consulting. She is the co-founder and Executive Director of Greater Works Foundation, a non-profit organization that provides outreach to underprivileged, under-served, and underrepresented youth and communities by promoting financial literacy, educational enrichment, leadership skills, mentoring, and global service initiatives that will cultivate the next generation of responsible leaders thereby creating empowered citizens and communities.

A woman with a passion and gift for strategic prayer and intercession, **Juarkena** authored *Speak Life: 101 Faith Building Affirmations* to kick-start and undergird the everyday believer's prayer life.

To contact **Juarkena Pitts**, email info@juarkenapitts.com. For additional information, please visit www.juarkenapitts.com.

# Every Decision Matters
## By: Danielle Evans

In the life of an entrepreneur every decision matters. Why? You ask? It can ultimately determine the life and longevity of your business. I like to think of decision making as the thought process of selecting a logical choice from all available options while being open to change and visiting uncharted territory. Visiting uncharted territory or as I like to call it - stepping into the dark side, is simply moving out of your comfort zone and out of the norm. It can be the most challenging and the most rewarding for your business. As an entrepreneur I make it a habit to weigh the positives and negatives of each option, and consider all alternatives. I've grown to learn that the intensity and impact of a single decision, has the power to assist, elevate or in some cases, destroy a business. That is why all options have to be examined. *Sam Walton's decision to hold Saturday morning all-employee meetings led to a culture of rapid information and decision-making, which in turn created one of the biggest companies in the world. Samsung's decision to launch a sabbatical program that sends top talent all around the world continues to be the secret behind their success as a global brand. In contrast,* Kodak instantly recognized the potential of the device to revolutionize photography and invested billions in its development, but conservative forces within the company stalled the release of a digital camera, afraid to abandon the film-and-paper product line that had brought it untold riches. By the time Kodak finally shifted to digital in the late 1990s, the megapixel revolution had long passed it by. Kodak filed for Chapter 11 bankruptcy protection and announced that it was dropping its failed digital camera line entirely. These are just a couple of examples of how every decision matters in any size business and how it can change the impact and outcome of a business.

Starting my journey as an entrepreneur in my late 40's, while always having held a steady secure job for twenty years in the airline industry, took a huge leap of faith and patience. It was a life changing decision especially not knowing how all the pieces worked. I knew how to provide stellar service to people but I didn't know the business aspects. Things that were new to me included, the public relations aspect, the different avenues of advertising, bookkeeping, and hosting events. This would all be a venture into the dark side. In the beginning, I would spend my time attending free classes on YouTube, Facebook, Periscope and other media outlets, piecing together how to run my business. By choosing to utilize social media as a method of educating myself, I was in business without any business. Working to educate myself this way would always get me to the starting line but never in the race. The instructors were knowledgeable, gave good nuggets, and only provided selective information. In looking to save money by using the least expensive avenues I was restricting myself to a one-way street to nowhere. I became stagnant in growth and momentum, I was only receiving bits and pieces of information when in actuality I needed the whole pie in order to get the full picture of how I was going to succeed in this entrepreneurial world. Sadly, my business almost ended before it began.

Understanding that I needed to make a dramatic 360-degree decision to save my business, I began entertaining the thought of hiring a coach or coaches, reviewing their success rates, and how to build that into my newly created budget that didn't officially exist until now. In deciding to hire a business coach, it was one of the best decisions I've ever made. That one major decision forced me to focus, gave me direction and clarity and most importantly, it allowed me to truly generate income.

My journey of entrepreneurship has been exciting, overwhelming, and fulfilling all at the same time and sometimes in the same day. There have been so many lessons I've learned concerning the power of decision making that has affected my business.

Here are a few **Entrepreneurial Keys for Success** that I would like to share with you:

- **Fly solo** – Decide that it is ok, if everyone is not on board. As an entrepreneur you have to believe when no one else believes and you have to see it when others visions are blurry.
- **The scales aren't always balanced** – You are going to have good days and bad days, profitable days and non-profitable days. Decide to make sure you have reliable accountability partners and daily goals set in advance to tip the scales. I have a daily goal to accomplish 3 small tasks, 1 medium task and 1 large task in order to produce strides in my business.
- **Go big or go home** – Decide to be an action taker by researching all angles and possibilities, then go from intention to inception, throwing caution to the wind.

- **Want more because there is more** – You can't out give God.
- **What you choose today affects your tomorrow** – Make conscious intentional decisions concerning your business daily.
- **Set high standards** – Decide not to settle for just enough, go for the gold and win big in your business.
- **Don't lose tomorrow on yesterday** – Let go of past actions that resulted in bad business decisions. Don't become paralyzed. Learn from past actions and move forward.
- **Get off the crazy cycle** - Stop making the same decisions that didn't work over and over, trying to push or force change. This is known as insanity and will give entrepreneurs false hopes.
- **Change is good** – Understand that what has been sustaining you in your business will not put you in overflow.
- **You will win if you don't quit** – Decide to make a conscious decision that quitting is not an option.

**Danielle Evans** Your Favorite Vision Coach Extraordinaire, Life Mentor to Women, Empowerment Speaker, Author and Founder of Living in 3D, focuses on individuals who are in search of meaning, purpose and satisfaction in their life. She leads the everyday person to discover their God given gifts, develop those gifts, and use those gifts to walk into their destiny with purpose. She speaks to a diverse group of individuals as a speaker on various panels and through Living In 3D, a platform she created to enlighten and empower others to have effective action towards their destiny with intentional movement.

    With an honest and open delivery, Danielle Evans gives new perspective, by shedding surmounting excuses and injecting massive amounts of facts and truths. Her engaging and transparent approach is freeing and her commitment to bring you the very best of what she is living and learning is inspiring. Danielle's vision is for you to use your gifts to release fulfillment, happiness, and success so that you can begin to receive what's DUE YOU.

Danielle Evans is the wife to Craig Evans, mother to 3 adult children, 3 grandchildren and a native of Birmingham, AL. Connect with Danielle at www.danielleevansin3d.com or email danielle@danielleevansin3d.com.

# The Power of Prayer – A Quiet Mind

By: Ronda A. White

Prayer is my personal HERO. Prayer is a means of connecting to God's undying love, presence, direction, and provision. Connecting with my Heavenly Father for wisdom, direction, and guidance has been my biggest WIN in life. Prayer is not just asking for HELP but glorifying God and desiring a relationship with Him. The bible spells this principle out to each of us in The Lord's Prayer found in the bible in the 11th chapter of Luke verses 2 - 4. While prayer is also an expression of gratitude and a form of worship, it should also be a source for direction, guidance, and encouragement.

After prayer, I am rejuvenated and at peace with the task that follows and the part I play in it.

Forest Gump said, "Life is like a box of chocolates, you never know what you're going to get." Life is full of setbacks, fear, failure, limitations, and disappointments. These are all a part of the journey. How you respond to the distractions and challenges in business can make or possibly break you and your bank account. Life was not designed to be perfect, hence the reason we have options. Our need to succeed, do well, and be accepted in our space presents each of us with other types of challenges. How do you handle all the pressure? On my journey I have learned not to be reactive but instead be quiet, where I quiet my mind, soul, and spirit and center myself through prayer.

Prayer allows me to believe that all things are possible. The answer I am seeking through prayer may not happen in my timing, but prayer gives me the peace and stability to be patient while in expectation. What I love about prayer is that I can simply be me. I can share from my heart by expressing any hurt, disappointment, or frustration. I don't have to use any fancy wording or formulate any type of decree. I simply talk to God as well as listen. There are times when I go to pray and I don't have any words to say. At that point, I choose to pray in the spirit or be quiet. In that respect, prayer silences me and removes me from the equation.

Prayer also helps me remain grounded as it is the foundation of both a personal and business goal that I maintain daily. My personal goal is to work voluntarily vs. obligatorily. Another personal goal I have is to help others to make a difference in their community as well as in this world. Prayer gives me the gift of calmness. It allows me the insight not to pick up extra unnecessary baggage (learning to say no).

It is so easy to become overwhelmed as an entrepreneur, believing you have to wear all the hats: CEO, visionary, office manager, operational manager, human resource manager, customer service manager, CFO, and sales manager. Whether you have a team or not, you just began in business, or are a seasoned entrepreneur, you will learn that you do not have to wear all of those hats and you will still face many challenges in business. When I am faced with those challenges, I am reminded that I am not the 'true' owner of my business. With prayer as the foundation and listening to His counsel, my God is the true owner. He continually asks me to execute His orders. In response, my productivity level in business has been more than elevated.

Allow me to share a simple truth that I want all that read this to avoid. As a new full-time entrepreneur I was doing it all and doing it all wrong. If the phone rang, I stopped what I was doing to answer it. If I got an email or inbox on Facebook, I was quick to answer and provide stellar customer service as this could be a potential client. I became overwhelmed and begin staying up late just to get work done when it was quiet between 1am and 4am. I was giving up my sleep and self care just to handle business. I remembered being so tired and thinking, what is going on? I am more organized than this, but it wasn't about organization. It was really about my process and procedures. I lost control of my day, my time, and my work. I had to immediately silence my mind and ask for guidance.

My business wasn't yielding anything productive at this time. I knew in my heart, that God didn't give me this vision of failure. I needed a new plan in order to succeed. I rescheduled everything on my calendar on Wednesday of this particular week and I spent the whole day in silence. Praying, praising Him, reading and meditation on His word, I sat and listened. Almost immediately, God revealed to me a new working strategy for my day-to-day operation.

Another time, I had a huge decision to make on the direction of my business in relation to a huge contract I had received. I was only 3 days into my entrepreneurial journey and a little nervous. Alternatively, I was very excited and ready. We were halfway through the process. I extended great service and worked the contract by the terms defined, yet my client was not as forthcoming. It caused us to come to a mutual decision to sever the contract. My first 30 days and I was already shy of my set goal. How was I going to handle this challenge? I got quiet and prayed. What was revealed to me was everyone would not be the ideal client even when they fit the profile. We sometimes have to walk away. There is a big difference between what is good and what is right. With my integrity intact, I chose and will always choose what is right. That was a huge life lesson very early on.

In closing, remember prayer is your source of life and sometimes it requires your silence. Below I have shared my top 10 personal guidelines that helped me to get it done everyday in my business.

My top 10 **Entrepreneurial Keys for Success**:
- Dedicate your business back to God because it's His anyway.
- Speak the Word of God over your business.
- Pray for your business and clients.

- Twice a month – (Wednesday is my day). NO work. I get quiet all day with the Lord in prayer, reading, praise, and meditation.
- Set your day up the night before.
- Work in 90 minute blocks (yes I set a timer).
- Take breaks after the blocks (I take 30 minutes)
- Turn off all social media alerts during block time.
- Schedule the time to learn more about your industry and what's new and fresh.
- Schedule time off each quarter to personally rejuvenate.

Master Life and Business Optimizer, Radio Host, International Speaker, Author and President/Founder of The R.A.W. Group LLC., a consulting firm assisting others in life and business through coaching, training and workshops. She is the operational and programmatic fuel beginning behind the movement I AM P.A.T.E.N.T.™ and desires for all to walk in their truth according to the Word of God.

Known for her brilliance as a consummate life and business strategist, Ronda chases and defines growth opportunities, in any capacity, with a fervor that is unmatched. Her sharp insight enables her to unravel the fabric of your vision – startup or seasoned – adeptly shifting snags into solutions. Ronda is ignited daily by her purpose to not just inspire but to empower. She amplifies her message on every medium within her grasp.

She is also the Co-Founder of A Black and White Affair – leading women into healing from the black and white areas in their life. Ronda currently volunteers as an Advisor Board member for SAFY of Oklahoma and she's a member of Toastmaster International Local Conoma Chapter in OKC where she resides.

To connect to Ronda A. White or for additional information visit www.rondaawhite.com or email ronda@rondaawhite.com.

# I Said, "YES"

## Overcoming Struggle with a Changed Mindset
### By: Cassandra Goodman

The Urban Dictionary defines a positive mindset as a healthy way of thinking that produces harmony and good results. The thought process is in direct alignment with success. Many entrepreneurs fail to realize the effect of not having balance in their professional and personal lives. The two are intertwined.

    I was always waiting for the perfect time to create products, to advertise my business, to connect with someone, or to begin planning things that had been in the back of my mind for months. I eventually had to deal with my reality. Once I did, I was able to put procrastination and my fears in check. What a difference a changed mindset makes. I was relieved and able to move forward from what was holding me back.

Your personal life, in some ways, duplicates your professional life. If you are unhappy in your personal life, most likely you will also be unhappy in your professional life. Many entrepreneurs work a lot of hours to avoid dealing with their money issues, marital issues, children acting up, coping with pain, chaos, and other dysfunctions going on in their personal lives. There has to be a balance. You must face these issues. Only you and God of course, can change that. What you don't want is to stand in your own way of success.

Going through a very toxic relationship hindered me from working in the field that I knew I was purposed to be in. As a result of remaining in that relationship, I was forced through mental, emotional, verbal, and physical abuse, which did not allow me the opportunity to be the best at what I knew I was capable of. I decided not to work in fear or live in complete chaos. I was so full of ambition and ready to take on the challenges of being able to help others. BUT wait, how could I help others when my life was a complete disaster? I felt stuck, confused, anxious, and disappointed. I felt stuck because I couldn't function in the dysfunction. I had so many ideas of things I wanted to do with my life but couldn't. Behind my smile was a lot of hurt and pain. I knew that I had to get my life together fast and in a hurry. I felt confused because I was trying to figure out why this person betrayed me so much with his threats and ill treatment. I felt anxious because I was living in complete fear of what could happen. I felt frustrated because my purpose was put on hold until I could get my life together. I was overwhelmed with it all. I just knew that I had to do something.

Through my faith, I realized that I was a victor and not a victim. I knew that I was not in this alone because I knew that God had my back through it all. I decided to remove myself from the situation and I knew that I had nothing to fear. If I can go through this and succeed, then so can you! Don't allow the curveballs life throws at you to alter your mindset. Things may be a little unsteady now, BUT we know that trouble doesn't last always. Sometimes it can be hard to keep a positive mindset, yet it is necessary.

So…

Breaking free was one of the best decisions I've ever made. From that moment forward, I decided that I will never allow ANYTHING to stop me.

**Break free from the chaos. Someone is waiting for you to share your greatness!**

Here are the **Entrepreneurial Keys for Success** I developed in order to change my mindset and break free:

- **Identify the problem.** You can't resolve a problem until you know what the problem is. Once you identify the problem, you are able to work on steps to eradicate the problem.

- **Accept the problem for what it is.** It is so important to clear your life of any unnecessary baggage. Especially if it doesn't align with who you are and where you are going. Many times, we will go into denial mode when we have a problem that we don't want to face. We want to have control of everything. Don't ignore it but accept it for what it is so that you can eliminate it and move forward.
- **Deal with the issue.** Sometimes it can be hard to face your truth. The consequence of not facing your truth is that you will remain stuck, frustrated, and confused on why you cannot reach your next level in your business. You will spend more time and energy going around the problem than facing it. Don't delay your success. If you have issues that you can't resolve alone, please seek professional help.
- **Move on.** Some days will be harder than others. Take one step at a time and you will eventually overcome. The problems we face

can either make us or break us. Keep going! The only way from here is up!

Affirmations I live by:

1. What you think is what you will become.
2. See the good in every situation. Mindset is everything!
3. Fear and faith don't mix. Choose wisely!
4. With faith, passion and a willingness to do what it takes, you can have anything in this world.
5. If it doesn't make you better, get rid of it.
6. It's all connected; your gifts, your circumstances, your purpose, your imperfections, your journey, and your destiny. It's molding you; embrace it!

Remember that your personal life reflects your professional/entrepreneurial life. Never allow the challenges you face to change your mindset. Sometimes you may not be able to see your way, but faith your way through! I do believe that you can overcome any obstacle with a changed mindset! Don't allow anything to stop you from reaching your next level of success!

Cassandra Goodman is a Life Transformation Coach, Bestselling Author, Writing Contributor, and the Founder of Women On a Move Association, a network that promotes positivity among women: advocating for women's rights, promoting leadership development, and providing community service.

Cassandra supports women in overcoming their fears, pains, and struggles, while assisting them in giving birth to their purpose. She believes that every person is equipped with everything they need to live a purposeful life with guidance and support. Cassandra is their source of support. Cassandra was recently chosen as one of South Carolina's Black Page's Top 20 under 40.

Cassandra is a Bestselling Author of "*I Am Woman: 21 Triumphant Women Sharing Their Journey to Embracing Truth and Their Authentic Self*" Volume I. She is also an online Writing Contributor for Rejoicing Hope Magazine, which helps women who are lost, hurting, and suffering in silence live a victorious life filled with hope by empowering them through the written and spoken word.

She is able to give back by volunteering her time by serving as co-chairperson of the South Carolina National Kidney Foundation Team. To contact Cassandra visit www.cassandraspurpose.com or email cassandraspurpose@gmail.com.

# Trusting In My Source And Not My Resources

By: Tamiko Kelley

A principle that I use in business is trusting in my source and not my resources. My source is the creator of heaven, and earth. He is King of kings, and LORD of lords. My source is the One who made man in His own image; made in His likeness. He placed in me intrinsic worth, purpose, destiny, and a measure of faith. In the beginning of creation, He made provision for man before He created him. He never intended for me to live my life totally independent apart from him. My source is God.

It is important not to totally trust in your resources. Don't trust in your money, bank accounts, property, or possessions. You may own houses, land, cars, trucks, a boat, a business, capital, assets and all of the inanimate objects you can think of, yet, never put your trust in only those things as it can create a serious problem. When we trust in things, money (riches or wealth) *only*, it typically results in having a false sense of security. What if you lose your job or the company shuts down? Will you be able to support yourself and your family if that income stops? Will you lose your home or car? Will it cause your lifestyle to change? Can you handle it? Not everyone can. Some become destructive and take their anger out on others. The way that a person views a matter certainly makes a difference in the direction he or she may take going forward. One door may be closing while another door of opportunity may be opening up on the other side.

Let's take a look at my story.

My job ended with a company of which I was an employee for eight years. It doesn't matter how, or why it ended. The end result is that I was unemployed. My responsibilities didn't go away due to this unexpected loss. I still had a mortgage as well as a household to provide for. I am the sole provider. Keep the principle in mind as this story unfolds.

The water is off in my entire neighborhood. If the people around me in my area have no water, my water should be off too. I double-checked to make sure that the bill was paid (I knew that it was). I asked a couple of people in my home if the water was off. Of course the response was, no. It is not off! I began turning on the faucets in my home to check if I still had good running water. There was no air in the pipes. There was no appearance of contaminated water flowing. The water appeared clean and filtered. In fact, there were no signs that my water was ever off. My mind focused on God. I believe in my heart that God kept my water supply flowing. More than a year later I was doing just fine. My lights and water have never been disconnected because I didn't pay the bills. I still had my home and car.

During this time, I am still unemployed and was continually seeking employment. Eventually I was hired at a daycare center. I was hired as a fill-in. As a fill-in, I only work, as needed, when teachers are out of work. How often depends on the true need of the daycare. While working there at the daycare center, I met the parent who became my first client in the cleaning business. I could never have imagined that job would lead to me starting my own business. You see, cleaning is my passion. What began as a small step of allowing myself back into the workforce eventually became a sprouting business. My business started growing exponentially by word of mouth. The years have been passing by and my cleaning business has been doing great.

Simultaneously, things began taking a downward turn in the US (United States) economy. Gas prices were increasing like I had never seen before. America was in a recession. Many things were happening during this period of time. When I would look at the news on television, I heard talk about the unemployment rate, trouble in the housing market, auto industries, banks, people losing their homes, and savings spent. During this time, I had clients that cut back.

In my mind, I am thinking that having a housekeeper is to have a luxury in many cases. It is simply not a necessity. I am told that I need to find a job. Why should I go and find a job in the workplace? I continue trusting in my source. This is a time period that I operate in the principle of trusting in my source, and not my resources. I am taking my chances with what I have. My safe place, my trust is in my source. My business survived those hard times and thankfully we are still thriving in the year 2017.

**Entrepreneurial Keys for Success** I invite you to implement if you are a service provider or simply when facing fear or financial hardship:

- Trust God with your resources. He gave you the ability to do what you do. Give tithes, and offerings into the kingdom of God. He gives the increase.

- Be the best at what you do.
- Make sure that both you and your clients or customers are satisfied.
- Don't take advantage of the people you serve in order to gain a profit even in financial hardship or a crisis.
- Pray concerning your business affairs and seek God for direction by the leading of Holy Spirit when making decisions.
- Don't allow your customers or clients to take advantage of you or cheat you.
- Don't cheat yourself when faced with fear of not getting new clients. It is okay if you don't win them all over for business when you can't reach a mutual agreement. Know your own worth.
- Know when and when not to increase prices or rates, especially when there is economic hardship in the country.

Tamiko Kelley is the Founder and CEO of Just Maid For You, a cleaning service that provides convenience and cleanliness to families and businesses, whether the service is a necessity or a luxury. Tamiko values people and work, therefore she's built a great reputation for good quality work, consistency, dependability, and respect. She enjoys the simple, and yet important things in life like family, friends, ministry, and encouraging and helping others. To connect with Tamiko Kelley email tk.kelley12@gmail.com.

# Destiny and Decisiveness, My Destiny Is In My Hands!

By: *Jacqueline Battle*

*Destiny,* by my definition is a determined mind focused on getting you to your place of purpose. Getting started by being *decisive* is the key to your destiny. Often times we sit on ideas too long and waste precious years thinking: *Shall I start the business now, or wait until the kids get out of school, or wait until the time is right, or wait until I save enough money?* Most of the time we allow circumstances to hinder us from moving forward. In actuality, we are dealing with fear. Fear is procrastination in disguise and it keeps you second-guessing yourself. Procrastination always says, "Wait until a better time or opportunity." It prevents us from being decisive, which, in turn, prevents us from reaching our goals and fulfilling our destiny.

*Deciding* is the beginning of a transformed life. I have learned to be decisive through trials and tribulations experienced in my life. On the opposite end, to be *indecisive* hinders you from moving forward toward your goals and your destiny. My destiny is in *my* hands, not anyone else's. At any given time, we are only one decision away from something different, from something new - from changing our lives.

It was in February of 2015 when the owner of the local real estate firm I worked for announced that he would be releasing those of us who were not generating enough sales. I was one of those who was released. I was a little disappointed to find myself included on that list. You see, I am also a real estate investor, which took up most of my time. This left little time to sell real estate. Being released from the real estate firm was the motivation I needed to open my own company. I politely handed in my documents and keys and I made the decision to register to take the broker's class online. I had been in real estate since 2006. As a result, I had more than enough time invested to qualify to start my own brokerage firm.

I studied continuously day and night. Being determined and aggressive, I passed the online exam as well as state exam within 45 days after registering for the class. I subsequently opened my own real estate firm in May of 2015. It was with pleasure that I decided to send my former employer the announcement that I had received my broker's license and I was opening my own firm. It gives you great joy to know that you have accomplished a goal, a dream, and a vision.

The Word of God says that it is He who gives us the power to get wealth (Deuteronomy 8:18). Anything and everything we have is because of the goodness of God.

*If it is to be, it is up to me.*
- William H. Johnson

Another time I took my destiny into my own hands was when I decided to become an author. I have written three books: *Transformed, Transform Your Life Now,* and *Transforming Devotionals*. There is a certain grace that comes upon you once you have accomplished a certain task. After completing my first book, the grace was there to write the remaining two books within months of each other. The decision to write one book led to three books.

When I think back a little further, I can recall another time I took my destiny into my own hands was in 1994. I had recently become a Mary Kay representative, and wanted to attend the annual convention in Dallas, Texas. Being a young mother, I didn't have the finances to go. My sister (who recruited me) and I decided to have a yard sale. We sold clothes our children couldn't wear anymore. We sold everything and anything we could find that we weren't using or didn't need. We made enough money to attend our first convention, and we had enough to go on a shopping spree while in Dallas.

>*Where there is a will, there is a way.*
>     -    Author Unknown

Being decisive and working toward your destiny sometimes requires breaking the boundaries of fear and doubt. I mentioned earlier that I am a real estate investor. Becoming real estate investors was a big step for my husband and me. We decided to rent out our home for two years and moved into an apartment in order to buy our first investment property. At first, it was difficult to leave the comfort of our home, yet, we knew we had to do something different in order to transform our finances. From that one major decision, we now have seven investment properties.

The Word of God says in Philippians 4:13, "*I can do all things through Christ which strengths me.*" I am nothing without God. I can do nothing without Him. It was He that gave me the desire to study day and night to pass my broker's exam. It was He who gave me the tenacity and confidence to make decisions to reach my goals and fulfill my destiny. Our dependencies is totally upon God. Without Him, we can do nothing, and we will accomplish nothing.

Your destiny belongs to you. You are the one who decides whether to remain the same or transform your life. Whatever your reason for waking up every day, the deciding factor is YOU.

As you go about your daily life, remember these **Entrepreneurial Keys for Success**:
- Your destiny is in your hands.
- Your destiny belongs to you - no one else.
- You get to decide who remains or who leaves.
- You get to decide whether you will be an employee or an employer.

How bad do you want it?
What are you willing to do to achieve it?
If not now, when?

If everyone else can, why can't you?

You are reading this book because you made the *decision* to buy it. You are the determining factor in realizing that your destiny is in your hands.

I said yes! Will you?

Jacqueline Battle is the owner of Rent or Buy Real Estate Company, a Property Manager, Real Estate Broker and better known as Mrs. landlord among her tenants. She is the Founder and CEO of Women In Ministry TV, a "Live" online ministry that interviews Women in Ministry from around the world. She is the Founder of His Grace Ministries, an outreach ministry that hosts women conferences & sponsors a Feed My Sheep Distribution Program in Nigeria.

She studied Business Administration at Alabama State University. She is the author of three books and is writing her fourth.

She is married, a mother of two sons and one daughter in love. She is a conference host and speaker. Her motto - Life is Precious! Make it Count! Her main mission in life is to take as many people to heaven as she possibly can. Connect at rentorbuyrealestate@outlook.com or womeninministrytv@gmail.com.

I Said, "YES"

I AM
FOCUSED

# STAY CONNECTED

Yakinea Marie
Founder/CEO of
**I Am Woman Business Network**™

Corporate Office
1710 – 2$^{nd}$ Avenue North
Suite 209
Birmingham, AL 35203
(205) 518-6565

www.YakineaMarie.com
www.IAmWomanNetwork.com

## MEET THE AUTHORS

www.ISaidYes.biz

# I Said YES

Driven Entrepreneurs Who Overcame
Setbacks, Fear, Failure, & Limitations

# I Said YES

Driven Entrepreneurs Who Overcame
Setbacks, Fear, Failure, & Limitations

## 16 Driven Entrepreneurs in Collaboration with
## Yakinea Marie

Made in the USA
Middletown, DE
11 September 2022